# Beyond Darkness

## Words for Reflection

## Cliff Reed

The Lindsey Press
London

a unitarian publication

Published by the Lindsey Press
on behalf of The General Assembly of Unitarian and
Free Christian Churches
Essex Hall, 1–6 Essex Street, London WC2R 3HY, UK

© Clifford Reed 2021

ISBN 978–0–85319–095–0

Designed and typeset by Garth Stewart

# CONTENTS

# PREFACE

*........... beyond darkness*
*there is light, beyond sorrow there is joy,*
*beyond death there is life.*

Welcome to my latest collection of 'words for reflection'. The years
during which I wrote this book included some dark times, shadowed
by terrorism, environmental abuses, and, most recently, the Covid-19
pandemic. The title is taken from my response to that threat, written
at Eastertide in 2020. Such challenges to our faith and our optimism
require a response that is neither trite nor despairing. With these and
some other hard issues I have felt it necessary to engage.

The contents of the opening section were particularly written for use
in services of worship. They are followed by reflections on a wide range
of themes that have spiritual significance – for me at least, and maybe
for others too. The natural world has always had great significance
in my life, and the third section is devoted to it. The passing seasons
and their feasts and fasts come next, as they are part of all our lives.
Our passage through life – from birth to death – is the subject of the
following section. Places can come to occupy special niches in our
thoughts and memories, and I include my reflections on some that do
so for me. The 'Memorial' section is about people and events that have
affected me and – in some cases – a great many others.

Throughout the book there are pieces with a strongly personal
emphasis, and this is most true of the closing 'Testimony' section.
My justification for including this is Ralph Waldo Emerson's advice to
ministry students in 1838 that "The true preacher can be known by this,
that he deals out to the people his life" – and I have been a preacher for
a long time!

I hope you will find here something that is not only of interest but
also of use.

*Cliff Reed*
*Ipswich, Suffolk, January 2021*

# ABOUT THE AUTHOR

Cliff Reed was born in 1947 in London. His commitment to the Unitarian movement began in his teens. He became active in the Unitarian Young People's League and was its National President at the age of 20. He qualified as a librarian and went to Guyana with Voluntary Service Overseas. Back in Britain, he worked at Dr Williams's Library in London, and became a member at Golders Green Unitarian Church.

Called to ministry, he trained at Unitarian College, Manchester, and studied theology at Manchester University. In 1976 he began his 36-year ministry at Ipswich, along with service to two rural congregations in Suffolk. In 1992 he undertook an exchange ministry in Bloomington, Illinois. Always active in the wider Unitarian movement, he has served as Secretary of the International Council of Unitarians & Universalists, and as President of the General Assembly of Unitarian & Free Christian Churches. He retired in 2012 and was appointed minister emeritus by the Ipswich Unitarian Meeting.

He began writing devotional material as a student, contributing to several anthologies and three hymnals. His publications include *We Are Here* (Lindsey Press, 1992), *The Way of the Pilgrim* (Ipswich Unitarians, 1993), *Celebrating the Flame* (Van der Heijden Publishing, 1997), *Spirit of Time and Place* (Lindsey Press, 2002), *Sacred Earth* (Lindsey Press, 2010), *'Till The Peoples All Are One': Darwin's Unitarian Connections* (Lindsey Press, 2011), *Unitarian? What's That?* (Lindsey Press, 1999, 2011, 2017, 2018), and *Carnival of Lamps* (Lindsey Press, 2015).

# WORSHIP

## HERE TO LOVE

We are here to love –
to love each other,
to love our frail, wounded selves,
to love our broken world,
and to love its suffering people.
Let us worship so that
love will flow.

## FLAMES FOR PEACE

We kindle our chalice flame
as other chalice flames burn brightly
around the world.
May our flames
warm all human hearts
of all faiths and nations
and direct us towards a future
of peace and justice,
oneness and loving kindness.
May it be so!

## GIVE THANKS FOR LOVE

*... for God is love* (I John 4: 8)

Give thanks for love. Real love,
not something vague, unfocused, abstract...

Real love: love as heartbreak,
love as consuming passion,
love as suffering with, for, and because of the beloved.

Give thanks for love.
Love as hot pumping blood,
as intimate caress, warm kiss, and tender touch;
love as the ecstasy of union –
physical, spiritual, transcendental.

Give thanks for love.
Love that forgives without reserve,
that bears no grudges;
love that carries no resentment,
no arrogance, no jealousy;
love that conducts itself with kindness,
gentleness, and humility.

Give thanks for love.
Love as the caring that reaches out
to someone who needs it,
welcoming, enfolding, healing,
protecting, and defending them;
love as laying down your life for them,
if that's what it comes to,
and it sometimes does.

Give thanks for the love that costs,
as well as the love that delights,
because that is what true love really is.

## TWO KINDS OF RELIGION

There are two kinds of religion in the world:
true religion and false religion.

Religion with love at its heart is true.
All other religion is false,
whatever its claims and dogmas.

May our religion be true.
May it be true because it is
loving, merciful, and kind.
That's all that matters.

## PRAISING GOD

(I Corinthians 13: 1–3)

It's fun to stand around praising God
with your like-minded friends –
it's easy.

What isn't so easy is to really think
about what you're doing, to ask if
all that praising really means anything.
Couldn't it just be a way of turning yourself on,
a 'feelgood' drug – albeit a safer one than most?

And it isn't easy to really think
about who or what you're praising.
Is there anything there,
apart from your own wishful thinking?

Isn't all that praising really about *not* thinking?
But neither praising nor thinking
means anything without loving –
which is what really matters.

Praising without loving is empty noise.
Thinking without loving is soulless calculation.
So let's praise God and think and love –
but above all, love.

Now let's all take time to think about that,
and praise God that we can!

## BROOM OR TIMESHIP?

You could say that a family is like a favourite broom.
Sometimes you replace the brush,
sometimes you replace the handle,
but through the years it's the same old broom.

In the family, people wear out and fade away
to who knows where, but new people come along
in one way or another, and the love remains.

You could say we are the crew of a timeship,
travelling forwards into mystery – because a
timeship has no reverse. We come aboard,
we play our part, we leave, our duty done.

But the family timeship sails on
before the fair winds of love...

May it be so!

## FOR THE MARTYRS

I pray for all who are suffering oppression
and torture because of their religion,
all who have become martyrs at the hands
of cruelty and malice masquerading as faith.

I pray that those in the grip of evil
 and blasphemous ideologies will repent
of their great folly and turn again
to the right path of God and of humanity.

And if they won't, I pray that they will be defeated,
and their structures of injustice utterly destroyed,
lest they dig themselves still deeper
into whatever hell they serve.

I ask this in the name of all God's messengers.
Amen.


## GOING DOWN HOPING

We're going down.
The world is in a tailspin.
Our beautiful earth is headed for destruction,
along with us, its foolish people.
Yes, we're going down,
going down in flames.

And yet, and yet...
we're going down hoping.

And because there's hope,
maybe we can catch ourselves
and our world in time.
Maybe we won't go down after all.
Let's hope so.
Let's make it so!


## CARPE DIEM

*... for the Reign of God is now in your midst.* (Luke 17: 21)
(James Moffat's translation, revised edition, 1934)

*Above us only sky.* (John Lennon, 'Imagine', 1971)

Don't wait for God to come down and save you,
that ain't gonna happen!

Wake up to the Divine within you and save each other
from life's cruelty as best you can.

If you can do that, then you might just
save yourselves.

But if saving yourself is all that concerns you,
then you're wasting your time – and your life.

The Kingdom of God is
within you,
among you,
between you –
not above you.

## INCARNATION

*... Certainly this was a righteous man.* (Luke 23: 47)

God doesn't "come down" from "up there"
and, once or twice, "put on" the human form.
There is no such God as that, except in myth.

But sometimes there are human beings
in whom we, their sisters and brothers,
see a quality we may call "divine",
and we dub them "avatars" or some such name as that.

But what we mean is this:
that what is true of all of us –
what could, what should, be true of all of us –
is made manifest in their struggle and their courage,
their wisdom and their loving kindness.

This is where God is,
this is what God is,
always within us,
always among us,
always incarnate.

But it takes someone special to reveal it,
and it takes clear perception to see it.

Open our eyes to the Kingdom that is already here,
calling us to enter and to love.
May it be so.

## UNCERTAIN WORLD

In a world that is uncertain,
where all our plans may be swept away at any moment,
we can put no trust in the structures we erect,
the structures we inherit.
If they are all that we bequeath,
then we are bequeathing nothing that will last.

But we are human beings who have found in each other
a community of values.
It is these that unite us, inspire us, move us.
It is the love which underlies them that gives us
joy in one another, that gives us what strength we have.

As we face the tumults that await us,
that will make our plans as meaningless as any
that human beings have ever made,
we dedicate ourselves to the values
that make us truly human –
humble before the Infinite,
humble before each other's deepest needs,
humble before the glory
and the terror of Creation.

We draw on our fund of values
and offer one another
what strength we have – and, in love,
we offer the world what we have found.

## SALVATION

What shall I do to be saved?

Saved from what?

Hell? It doesn't exist,
except where we have made it.

The Devil? He doesn't exist either,
except in human hearts,
especially those which suppose themselves
the most righteous.

The World? It is the world that
needs saving – from us.

Death? Save us, not from timely death
but from untimely old age and its decay;
from the delusion of immortality,
from clinging on to dotage
when the time has come to let go.

Then it is the Reaper whom our Saviour sends
to save us from life's cruellest mockery.

# THE PREACHERS' PRAYER

*Oh preacher won't you paint my dream,*
*won't you show me where you've been,*
*show me what I haven't seen to ease my mind.*
(Cat Stevens, 'Tuesday's Dead', 1971)

*The true preacher can be known by this, that he deals out to the*
*people his life – life passed through the fire of thought.*
(Ralph Waldo Emerson, 'The Divinity School Address', 1838)

Spirit of prophecy,
make us true preachers of the Word,
true preachers of what life has taught us,
true channels of the truth we have learned
in fear and trembling.

Spirit of life,
make us true interpreters of our own lives,
true learners and true teachers
of what they have taught us –
in both their darkness and their light.

Spirit of reason,
make us true thinkers, with minds on fire;
make us true expounders of thought,
both our own and that which the wise have taught;
may we inspire others to think for themselves.

*(continued overleaf)*

Spirit of love,
make us messengers
of hope and of compassion,
may our words bring comfort to the sorrowful,
challenge to the complacent,
light to the benighted,
and a liberating smile
to the hard of face and heart.

Spirit of adventure,
be with us on the journey.
Make us true companions
to those who share the road;
true guides when it is given us
to know the Way.

## HOW DO WE GROW?

*We need more Rock'n'Roll in our churches!*
(Brixton Unitarian Young People's League, 'The Young Unitarian', 1958)

How do we grow as a community of the liberal faith?

There have been so many schemes, so many calls
to set in train some hopeful "big idea".

All have fallen short, at least in their well-meant stated aim.
So what to do?

We must keep on keeping on ...

Nurturing the local, because that is where we grow
when we do grow;
doing what works in our own localities,
sensitive to their nature and their needs.

Being ready to welcome the visitors,
the seekers, the pilgrims, the refugees –
because they *will* come if our doors
and our hearts are open wide.

(And don't forget the rock'n'roll!)


## THE INHERITORS

We are the inheritors.
We inherit the faith and the traditions
of those who were here before us.

We inherit the fruits of their struggle,
the legacy of their suffering,
the achievements of their courage,
the bounty of their generosity,
the afterglow of their vision.
We inherit as a unity the mingling of their diversity.

We inherit the Spirit that brings all things to be,
moulding purpose out of chaos
through the power of creative love.

We, the inheritors, give thanks
for all that we have received.

*(continued overleaf)*

But we who inherit must also bequeath.
May our bequest to our successors be all
that we have found of joy and compassion,
all that we have found to be divine.

And may the people of tomorrow be blessed
by what we leave them.


## SPIRIT OF PROPHECY

*I will pour out my Sprit on all mankind; and your sons and
daughters shall prophesy.* (Acts 2: 17)

May the spirit of prophecy be with us –
the spirit that speaks out against cruelty,
corruption, and injustice,
the spirit that speaks truth to power,
the spirit that isn't cowed
by the bullies, bombasts, and tyrants.
May the spirit of prophecy be with us –
speaking out for this planet and its myriad creatures,
calling us and all people to reverence and protect
the cycles of nature.
May the spirit of prophecy be with us –
poured out upon Earth's sons and daughters,
upon young women, young men, and all
who dream dreams of wholeness, beauty, and peace.
May it be so.

# OUR LOVE

O God of
all times,
all space,
all universes,
carry our love
to all whom we love
and have ever loved,
to all whom we have
never loved,
and bless them with it.
Amen.

## ADVENT COMMUNION

We gather in Advent to anticipate the season of the Nativity, the festival that will celebrate the coming of Jesus into the world.

For some he is Emmanuel, "God with us", the special presence of the Divine in a human being – come to save us from the darkness of our own sins.

For some he is a Prophet, who came to reveal God's path to righteousness and paradise.

For some he was a sage, a story-teller, a rebel, speaking truth to unjust power.

*(continued overleaf)*

We gather to anticipate once more the stories of his birth –
two stories woven into one, wrapped in myths and symbols
that few now understand. But the story has been ours since
childhood, and we will feel its warmth as we hear and sing
it yet again: Mary and Joseph's journey to Bethlehem, the
angels and the shepherds, the star and the wise men, the
birth of Jesus in the stable of a crowded inn. And, if we read
on, the slaughter of the children, the flight of the refugees ...

But now, in Advent, a reading for this time of anticipation:

*Reading from Luke 1: 26–38, 39–56, 67–79*

Soon we will be immersed in preparations for Christmas,
preparations that can squeeze out of our consciousness what
it's really all about. So now we pause, ahead of the mayhem,
to call to mind what Advent really is: a time of preparation
for the brightest Christian festival of all, when light shines in
the darkness, and hope is reborn in a world that seems short
on hope.

For the fortunate, the pleasures and fellowship of the table
are a part of Christmas, with food and wine a-plenty. And
Jesus, when he grew up, enjoyed food and wine with all sorts
of people, not all of them "respectable", as his critics and
enemies pointed out! And he also broke bread and drank
wine with his friends, symbols of their fellowship as one body
sharing one spirit.

On the night of his betrayal, the night before his death on the cross at the hands of those who feared him, he broke bread and drank wine with his friends for the last time before their fellowship was broken. And that last meal is what we remember now, as we break bread and share the cup of wine. The bread is a symbol of fellowship, of the body that we are, the continuing body of Christ. We share it in remembrance of him, as he said we should. *[The bread is broken and shared]*

The wine is a symbol of the life-giving spirit that filled Jesus, flowing in his blood, and which was poured out to fill his continuing body. We share it in remembrance of him, as he said we should. *[The wine is poured and shared]*

Let's say together the prayer that Jesus taught his disciples: *Our Father, who art in heaven, hallowed be thy name. Thy kingdom come. Thy will be done on earth as it is in heaven. Give us this day our daily bread. And forgive us our trespasses, as we forgive them who trespass against us. And lead us not into temptation, but deliver us from evil. For thine is the kingdom, the power, and the glory, for ever and ever, Amen.*

Divine Spirit, who dwelt in Jesus, be with us as we prepare for the festival of his birth. May we see to its heart but not disparage the celebrations, because we need them in a darkened time. And may we open our hearts to the timeless message of peace and goodwill, for we and the world need it.

May it be so. Amen. Go in peace.

## LENTEN COMMUNION
(With readings from William Tyndale's New Testament of 1526)

From Mark I:
*And it came to pass in those days, that Jesus came from
Nazareth, a city of Galilee: and was baptised of John in Jordan.
And immediately he came out of the water and saw the heavens
open, and the holy ghost descending upon him like a dove. And
there came a voice from heaven: Thou art my dear son, in whom
I delight. And immediately the spirit drove him into a wilderness:
and he was there in the wilderness forty days, and was tempted
of Satan, and was with wild beasts. And angels ministered
unto him.*

From 1 Corinthians XIII:
*Though I speak with the tongues of men and angels, and yet
had no love, I were even as a sounding brass: and as a tinkling
cymbal. And though I could prophesy, and understood all
secrets, and all knowledge: yea, if I had all faith so that I could
move mountains out of their places, and yet had no love, I were
nothing. And though I bestowed all my goods to feed the poor, and
though I gave my body even that I burned, and yet have no love,
it profiteth me nothing.*

**PRAYER:** In Lent we will remember the privations of Jesus in
the wilderness. And we will remember also his path towards
suffering and death in Jerusalem.

May we, in thought and prayer, reach out to those in the
wilderness today – homeless and in exile, in flight from war
and terror in their homelands, facing terrible dangers and a
doubtful welcome.

We hold in our hearts all those who are persecuted for their faith, whatever it may be. In particular, at this Lenten season, we pray for all those facing torture, rape, and murder because they follow Christ; suffering because of inhuman mockeries of faith that have no place for compassion or mercy or love.

As we meet for worship in safety and comfort, we pray for those who can't.

This we ask in the name of Jesus and all your messengers. Amen.

Now we celebrate communion, affirming our oneness – in time and space – with all who look to Jesus, be it as Messiah and Saviour, or simply as brother, teacher, and example to follow. We use the words of 1 Corinthians XI in William Tyndale's translation.

*For the Lord Jesus the same night he was betrayed, took bread: and thanked and break, and said: Take ye, and eat ye: this is my body which is broken for you. This do in the remembrance of me.*
(The bread is broken and shared)

*After the same manner he took the cup when supper was done saying: This cup is the new testament in my blood, this do ye as oft as ye drink it, in the remembrance of me.*
(The cup is filled and shared)

*For as often as ye shall eat this bread, and drink this cup, ye shall show the Lord's death, till he comes.*

*(continued overleaf)*

Let us join in saying the prayer of Jesus as it appears in Tyndale's translation of Matthew VI:

*O our father, which art in heaven, hallowed be thy name. Let thy kingdom come. Thy will be fulfilled, as well in earth, as it is in heaven. Give us this day our daily bread. And forgive us our trespasses, even as we forgive them that trespass against us. Lead us not into temptation. But deliver us from evil. Amen.*

CLOSING WORDS: *This is my commandment, that ye love together as I have loved you.* (John XV)

In that spirit let us go out in peace and love, taking with us to share all the blessings that we have found together here. Amen.

## SUNLIT SMOKE

Our time of worship ends.
We extinguish the chalice-flame
and maybe watch the sunlit smoke.

Our minds turn back to the here and now,
but for a while may our spirits linger
with the smoke, gently rising in beauty.

# REFLECTION

# GOD ISN'T ...

*God I've got to believe in you*
  *or live in death!*
  *Will you save us – all?*
    *Soon or now?*
  *Send illumination*
  *to our drowning brains*
  *– We're pitiful, Lord.*
  *We need yr help!*
(Jack Kerouac, 'Sea', *Big Sur*, 1960)

God isn't there for us to analyse,
to argue about and theologise over.

God isn't there for philosophy to debate,
for politicians to invoke,
or for preachers to prattle on about.

God isn't there to 'believe' or 'disbelieve' in,
to know or understand,
to speculate about or to discuss ad tedium.

God isn't in our words, our creeds, our books,
our theories, our trite affirmations, our empty cleverness.

God isn't there at all if what we really want is just
our own vanity splurged across the cosmos.

But God is there, whether we like it or not.
So live with it.

# ONE SMALL STEP

One Christmas an astronaut spoke to us from space.
He read to us from Genesis: "In the beginning
God created the heaven and the earth...",
and he greeted us all on "the good earth".

One July evening two astronauts landed on the Moon.
One called it, "One small step for man,
one giant leap for mankind".

We walked on another world. We saw earthrise.
We thought we could never be the same again.
Maybe some of us never were.

We gained perspective. We saw Earth's beauty
and fragility, realised the absurdity of our pride.

Science and technology, ingenuity and courage,
ambition and politics, money and resources
beyond imagination: these got us to the Moon.

These and the ambivalent human spirit,
"a little lower than the angels", reaching out
in both wonder and would-be mastery.

That was then, so many years ago.
We've drawn back, and the astronauts bide their time.
But the memory and the pictures remain,
the words from space,
earthrise ... and the perspective too.

*(continued overleaf)*

Let's reflect on them in quietness…

> O God, who made the lights in the firmament,
> we who once walked on the lesser light
> seek wisdom to walk this good earth
> in gentleness and peace.

## NEW EXODUS

No Moses leads them
to a promised land,
but still they come,
preyed on by parasites
without humanity.

They may number hundreds,
thousands, but they are not
a 'flood', a 'tidal wave',
they are people – each one
with their own story.

Still they come, in flight
from war and terror,
hunger and poverty –
desperate with hope.

Still they come, from lands
that cannot hold them
to a continent that offers
scant welcome.

Still they come, in wretchedness
and danger, seeking peace –
seeking a chance of food for all,
work for all, shelter for all.

Seeking the chance to prosper,
the chance for their children
not to die.

Still they come,
from blighted hate-ravaged countries,
from a continent of promise unfulfilled.

No Moses leads them,
but milk and honey
beckon just the same.
Still they come,
and we don't know what to do.

*Miserere.*


## RIDER OF THE RAINBOW

*Riders of the rainbow*
*let it grow, let it grow...*
(Paul Kantner, 'Your Mind Has Left Your Body', 1973)

There are days when I think
we don't deserve
the beautiful planet we live on.
I wonder what it would be like
to ride the rainbow to its apex
and then ride on ...                    *(continued overleaf)*

and maybe after a billion light years
to find another Earth as beautiful
as this one – but one with people
not sunk in greed and malice,
bigotry and hatred; people not bent on
cruelty and destruction
in the name of their idols and false gods.

But I don't suppose I ever shall.

There are days, though,
when I remember that those good people
are here, on this Earth, too.


## DEFENDERS

*Defend my fine forests, or our friendship falters.*
(*The Death of King Arthur*, translated by Simon Armitage, 2012)

This is our prayer, great friend.
Defend our forests, because they are burning,
because they are falling before a tide of greed and malice.

Defend their peoples
because they are threatened with genocide,
with the wilful destruction of their homes,
their societies, and their futures.
Defend the forests' myriad creatures,
the species that comprise their fragile ecosystems,
because there are those whose course is set on extermination.

Defend our forests
against those who are destroying them,
because we all need the breath of life
that trees create.
Defend our wetlands and our grasslands;
our over-fished oceans,
our poisoned rivers, and our polluted seas.
Defend our melting ice-caps and our shrinking glaciers.
Defend all the beauty and wonder of the Earth,
our only home.
And defend humanity against inhumanity,
against tyrants and autocrats,
and all who deny your people their right to live lovingly
and with dignity in peace and freedom.

We are asking you this because our hope is failing.
The world darkens, and we doubt our strength.
But we can't wait for miracles: the task is ours.
We must be the defenders for which we yearn.

So may this be our prayer, great friend:
grant us the fortitude and the wisdom
to defend the earth we love
and to cherish all whose lives are a part of it.

## DANCING TRANSCENDENTALLY

*Saturday afternoon,*
*people dancing everywhere,*
*shouting "I don't care".*
(Jefferson Airplane, 'Won't You Try / Saturday Afternoon', 1967)

It's a wet Saturday afternoon
and no one's dancing here,
although the music's playing.

Perhaps it's time to transcend
the bounds of space and time,
send out our spirits to merge
and mingle with each other –

with the joyous spirits of every age,
with the Great Spirit who danced
the universe into being.

And my special spirit will look out
for yours, and they could dance
and move together as our bodies
have never done and, maybe, never will.

I send you this with my love,
as one transcendent dancer
to another.

# MARY MAGDALEN – ROCK STAR

*Peter said to Mary, "Sister, we know that the Saviour loved you more than the rest of women. Tell us the words of the Saviour which you remember – which you know but we do not."* (Gospel of Mary)

Mary Magdalen wasn't a prostitute.
Lascivious, misogynistic churchmen
invented that particular lie
for unpleasant reasons of their own.

Mary Magdalen was a rock star,
who fell in love with Jesus
and blasted out his praises at gigs
from Tiberias to Jerusalem;
at festivals in springtime Galilee.

Mary Magdalen was no tame, submissive doormat either,
with downcast – or upcast – eyes.
Her twelve-strong band got things jumping.
Then we heard the voices of her vocal backing –
Joanna, Martha, and the girl they called 'The Virgin'.

It was time.
Mary Magdalen strode on stage and made it hers.
She seized the mike and sang.
God and the angel host came down to listen.

Eyes blazing, her voice soared amid guitar riffs.
She rocked the souls of thousands, come to share
their bread and fish on hillside and lakeshore.

*(continued overleaf)*

Then she paused. Smiled lovingly at someone
in the crowd – and Jesus stepped up to join her...

Is all this true?
Maybe not, but it's better than the lie the Church
has been telling for two thousand years.


## CHILDREN OF THE REFORMATION: A REFLECTION ON 500 YEARS

We are Protestants, children of the Reformation;
children of Martin Luther's protest,
which changed the world;
his demand that a rotting Church reform.

We are children of the Reformation's forerunners –
Wyclif and the Lollards in England;
in Bohemia, Jan Hus, whose chalice revolution
and death in flames we still remember in our worship.

We are children of Zurich's Reformation,
when Huldreich Zwingli gave us a simple memorial meal
in which to remember Jesus and his friends,
the bread and wine of human community
in place of priestcraft and superstition.

We are children of John Calvin's Reformation in Geneva,
his affirmation of the absolute Sovereignty of God the Father,
which helped others to say that 'God is One', and mean it.

We are children of the English Reformation,
of William Tyndale's courage in giving us the Bible
in our own tongue; of Thomas Cranmer's wordcraft
which gave the Reformed liturgy its English voice;
of Jane Grey's faith and martyrdom.

We are children of the Radical Reformation –
the Anabaptists and the Anti-Trinitarians
for whom the first Reformers didn't go far enough.

We are children-in-spirit of a brave and lonely Spaniard,
Michael Servetus, who proved too radical for Catholic
and Protestant alike and died a martyr in Geneva.

We are children of the Polish Brethren
and their community at Rakow; of their Catechism
and its architect, Faustus Socinus;
of Symon Budny's Lithuanians,
at once more radical and more pragmatic.

We are children of the Transylvanian Unitarians
and their first leaders – Francis David, their theologian,
John Sigismund, their king – apostles of tolerance
to Christians of every creed.

We are children of England's Unitarian pioneers –
John Biddle, prisoner of conscience,
William Manning in the restless Suffolk countryside,
and others too in the troubled seventeenth century,
upholders of God's Unity and human liberty.

*(continued overleaf)*

We are children of those who first proclaimed
the liberal faith in our islands' other realms –
Jenkin Jones in Wales;
in Ireland Thomas Emlyn and Henry Montgomery;
William McGill, William Dalrymple,
and William Christie in Scotland.

We are Protestants, children of the Reformation
and Dissenters from imposed 'orthodoxies' –
and we are still protesting, still reforming, still dissenting,
because love, humanity, and God require it.
And although we affirm our own faith,
we do not deny the freedom of anyone to believe
according to their conscience
and to worship in goodwill.

## OLYMPIC RETROSPECTIVE

*Read me the name of the Olympic victor...*
*where it is written on my mind,*
*for I owe him a sweet song and have forgotten it.*
(Pindar, Olympian Ode 10)

*At the games ... all the runners take part, though only one wins the*
*prize. You also must run to win.*
(I Corinthians 9: 24–25)

The first Olympiad that I remember
was Melbourne in 1956,
when Dawn Fraser parted the waters,
and Australia rejoiced.

In 1960 Abebe Bikila padded barefoot
down Rome's torch-lit Appian Way,
and we knew that Ethiopia, with all Africa,
was claiming her rightful place at last.

'64 and the Games, founded beneath one sacred mountain,
were held in the shadow of another – Fuji-san;
Ann Packer ran to gold, and golden Mary leapt
to long-jump victory in Tokyo.

Mexico City in '68, the year of revolutions;
clenched fists of Black Power shook the Games,
and Bob Beamon's amazing jump
spanned the world.

A Russian waif called Olga steals hearts,
Mark Spitz swims to seven golds,
but Munich in '72 was when Black September
brought murder to the Games.

In 1976, in Montreal, the boycotts begin;
first it's the Africans.
Nadia, Romania's child gymnast,
amazes and disturbs. What childhood was hers?

Moscow 1980: the Games where Alan Wells
and Daley Thompson, Coe, and Ovett,
received their golds under the Olympic flag,
and the Americans stayed at home.

*(continued overleaf)*

Rocket-man opens proceedings in LA,
but the Soviets won't come in '84.
Tessa and Fatima chucked their spears
and smiled their smiles atop the podium.

Seoul in '88, and everyone's there again at last;
Flo-Jo – so fast, so beautiful, is America's pride;
Ben Johnson – disgraced, disqualified,
is Canada's shame.

'92 in Barcelona, Olympic homage to Catalonia:
Linford is Britain's hundred-metres hero
and Sally hurdles to gold, wonder-woman
caped in the Union Flag.

"Georgia on my mind", sings Gladys Knight in '96,
and the Games have come to Atlanta;
Muhammad Ali, mighty Olympian, lights the flame,
Michael Johnson, golden-shod, runs to double gold.

The Games go south to Sydney in 2000;
Cathy Freeman kindles the flame,
then runs and wins for two Australias,
carries both their flags and makes them one.

2004 and the Games go home to Hellas:
in Athens, Kelly strides to two-fold victory
and can scarcely believe it herself,
eyes popping at the scoreboard!

A lightning Bolt from Jamaica
seared through Beijing's Bird's Nest;
it's 2008, when golden Rebecca swam to victory,

and a Chinese spectacle took our breath away.

The old Olympian gods smiled on London in 2012:
the greatest, golden Games, happy and glorious –
Jess, with a face as bright as Apollo's;
mighty, modest Mo;
and a Jamaican showman with wings on his heels.

2016 and it's Olympic Carnival in Rio!
Humanity is celebrated in a city
where the best and the worst flourish side by side.
British bikes, boats, and boxers
come home treasure-laden,
and there is even a hammer-throwing ballerina!

The athletes honed their bodies and their skills.
Tokyo prepared to welcome them,
and the world waited: but the venues –
stadium, pool, and all the rest –
stayed silent, empty. and unused.
Covid-19 struck the world's games in 2020.

## LOST LANDS

*... from her western shores*
*those beautiful sailors journeyed*
*to the South and North Americas with ease*
*in their ships with painted sails.*
(Donovan, 'Atlantis', 1968)

*(continued overleaf)*

*... there were earthquakes and floods of extraordinary violence,
and in a single dreadful day and night ... the island of Atlantis
was swallowed up by the sea.*
(Plato, 'Timaeus', 4th century BCE)

Myths, legends, and half-remembered stories
speak of lost lands, sunken cities,
engulfed by deluge and fire,
earthquake and volcano, tsunami and surging sea –
their proud and wilful peoples
destroyed by angry gods or vengeful nature.

Some of the stories are fantasies,
some have their roots in history.
They stand as testimony
to our planet's turbulence and power,
and sometimes to the devastation
that our own folly and hubris have unleashed.

May we be humble dwellers
on this blue–green Earth,
respecting her fertile soil and her living waters,
her forests, her grasslands, her wetlands
and all that lives in them,
dependent as we are on her bounty;
learning the folly of our polluting ways,
our casual despoiling of our only home,
the self-defeating nature
 of our greed, arrogance, and misrule.

The warnings are there – as much in science as in religion
or the truths of ancient myth.
Only fools deny them.

Let wisdom be ours, lest we follow
antediluvian humanity,
the builders of Babel,
the fabled over-proud Atlanteans,
and all the rest, into the shadows of decline and fall,
self-destruction and obscuring legend.


## IT IS NOT ENOUGH ...

*Bismillahir – Rahmanir – Raheem.*
*In the name of God the most merciful, the most compassionate ...*
*Guide us to the straight path.*
(The Qur'an 1:1, 6)

It is not enough to say that there is no god but God,
and that Muhammad or Jesus is his Prophet.

If you say these things and mean them,
then you must emulate, as best you can,
the mercy and the compassion that are God's.

If you say these things and mean them,
then you must never kill another believer,
you must never murder another human being.

If you say these things and mean them,
you must never unleash war and terror
on the innocent, never take up arms
except in their defence.

*(continued overleaf)*

If you say these things and mean them,
truly striving in the way of God,
then you will not give the name of 'jihad'
to a crime against humanity.

If you say these things and mean them,
 you must respect the honest faith and convictions
of other people and practise tolerance in religion.

If you say these things and mean them,
you must not arrogate to yourself
the divine prerogative of judgement,
 or presume to deal out justice in God's name.
God doesn't need your help – or anyone else's –
and neither do the Prophets, from first to last.

If, in God's name,
you do that which violates God's will
and the teachings of the Prophets,
you may stand charged as a blasphemer on the Last Day.

If, in God's name and in any way,
you treat another human being without justice,
mercy, or compassion,
then you have forsaken the straight path.

# DILEMMA

*For see! Where on the bier before ye lies*
*The pale, the fallen, the untimely sacrifice*
*To your mistaken shrine, to your false idol Honour.*
(Anne Finch, Countess of Winchelsea, 1661–1720,
from 'The Soldier's Death')

War is wrong.
We are sure enough of that, at least.
We will have no part in it, we say.
We will not kill or wound
a brother-man, a sister-woman.
To do so is a crime, perhaps the greatest crime.
And neither will we send our sons and daughters
to kill on our behalf.
We will not bomb or shell,
reduce cities to dust and blood.
No, rather we will sheathe the sword,
beat spears into ploughshares,
unmake the guns, the tanks, the warplanes;
make better use of warships, missiles, drones.
We will embrace our erstwhile foes,
make friends of enemies;
see God within them,
and love him there.
We will build peace with justice in the world.
Yes, war is wrong, we say,
and we forswear it.

*(continued overleaf)*

But for all our resolutions, guns still fire,
bombs still fall, mines still kill and maim.
*Someone* still makes war, still hates,
still brutalises; still rapes, still enslaves,
still unmakes humanity;
still chooses greed with violence,
pursues power without pity;
still tortures and murders
in the name of false gods and falsified religions;
still sacrifices men to "mistaken shrines",
women to that "false idol Honour".
The innocent, the helpless, and the weak
still suffer at cruel, contemptuous hands.
Who will free them and defend them if we do not?

Do we deceive ourselves that prayer
and pious words alone will be enough?
Do we set up our tender consciences
as yet more altars where humanity is sacrificed?
Could it be that war, though always wrong,
cannot always be avoided?

*Miserere.*

# WHO LIBERATED AUSCHWITZ?

*He that hath no sword, let him sell his garment and buy one.*
(Luke 22: 36)

*And the letters were sent by posts into all the king's provinces, to destroy, to kill, and to cause to perish, all Jews, both young and old, little children and women.*
(Esther 3: 13)

Who liberated Auschwitz?
Who liberated Dachau?
Who liberated Belsen?

Not the false prophets who cry
"Peace, peace" when there is no peace.

No, it was the Red Army,
the American Army, the British Army,
who put their lives on the line
to resist a monstrous evil and defeat it.

And where there is cruelty without conscience,
inhumanity without restraint,
with no finer feeling to appeal to,
is there really any alternative?

# AUGUST 4th 1914: THE FIRST FRUITS

*Dawn was theirs,*
*And sunset, and the colours of the earth.*
*... All this is ended.*
(Rupert Brooke, 1887–1915, from *1914 and Other Poems*)

The first fruits of a war's bitter harvest
are the first to be cut down, the first to fall.

Their deaths will say that here is no game,
no glory. Just an old folly replayed.

Together, as comrades, they face
a new reality: not all will go home.

And another: not all who do go home
will go with minds and bodies whole.

None will be unchanged.
But for now they are companions,
sharing bread on an uncertain road
whose ending they can't see.

And some never will.

# NATURE

## HAIL TO THE BLUE ...

*Bless the Lord, my soul. Lord my God you are very great ...*
*You have spread out the heavens like a tent ...*
*You take the clouds for your chariot, riding on the wings of the wind.*
(Psalm 104: 1–3)

Hail to the blue sky
and its white wisps of cloud.

Hail to the riotous green of springtime,
morphing into summer.

Hail to the daisies,
irrepressible worshippers of the sun.

Hail to the magpie strutting on the lawn,
the blackbird singing in the apple tree,
the crafty crows, the bold robin,
and all the other dinosaurs
who survived the cataclysm.

Hail to life triumphant and its Source,
whatever name we call it by.

Hail to humanity at its brilliant best –
and sorry about the worst.

# FRAGRANCE OF APPLES

The fragrance of apples conjures a dream
of blossom humming with bees,
singing with the voices of chaffinches in its midst;
of young apples forming, growing, ripening
from green to shades of russet and of red.

And then the harvest:
apples to eat as they are,
to cook in pies and crumbles;
apples to quench our thirst
as juice and cider.

For some another destiny:
to fall unpicked and be both home and larder
to insects and their young;
to be the food of blackbirds and wood mice,
end-of-season wasps,
drunk on rot and fermentation.

Then the leaves turn, fall:
the tree sleeps naked
but for its lichen-covered bark,
while we make merry with all it gave us
in another year of plenty.

## THE SACREDNESS OF TREES
*(Christchurch Park, Ipswich)*

*He was the King of Trees*
*Keeper of the glades ...*
(Cat Stevens, 'King of Trees', 1974)

In the middle of an oak grove,
with trees of a few years old and trees of centuries,
feel the sacredness, the everlasting power
of the life around you,
and know the transitory nature of your own.

The ancient druids, so it's said,
performed their secret rites in oak groves.
We don't know what they did
– which may be just as well –
but they found sacredness
among those ancient trees,
and so do we.


## INDIGO IN SUNLIGHT
*(Kalamazoo County, Michigan)*

Can there be
any greater beauty
than an indigo bunting
hopping out of shadow
into sunlight
by a forest trail
in springtime?

# TODAY IN THE FORUM

The forum, green and fragrant in the springtime, awaits.
Who will be the first to arrive, the first to claim a place?

Cautiously, among the blossom on display,
comes little Parus Caerulus, in his bright blue cap.
And then his bigger, bolder cousin, Parus Ater.

Next, all in black, sleek songster, Turdus Merula.
With portly, lumbering gait, Columba Palumbus
takes his place with every sign of prosperity,
pausing to drink from the public cistern.

Columba's cousins are here too – humble Livia from
the country, so often overlooked; and Streptopelia Decaoto,
descendant of immigrants from the east and clad still in
desert hues, but at home in the city for generations.

Bold Erithacus Rubecula, breast clad in martial red,
takes a defiant stand against all rivals for his pitch.
And with deceptive modesty, in demure grey and brown,
Prunella Modularis is on the lookout for illicit liaisons.

Fringilla Coelebs, in blue-grey cap and chestnut-pink,
is busy at the food-stalls, as are his colourful clan –
Chloris, all in green with yellow trim,
and gold-bedecked Carduelis.

Raucous, in an iridescent mob, comes Sturnus Vulgaris
and his gang. And then those archetypal plebs,
Passer Domesticus and her squabbling family,
each one counted by God.                    *(continued overleaf)*

47

Elfin-like the softly twittering company
of Aegithalos Caudatus passes through the crowd.
With roguish swagger, bold in black and white,
Pica Pica bounces in, closely followed
by Corvus Corone and his black-clad crew,
fearless of all save that occasional keen-eyed raider,
Accipiter Nisus,
whose thunderbolt arrival empties the forum.

## VAGRANTS

What happens to those vagrant birds
that get blown here on gales
or the tails of hurricanes?
Which arrive here, no one knows how,
from the far Americas or distant Asia,
turning up in our parks and gardens
to get the twitchers twitching?

What happens to them then?
Do they find their way home, like Odysseus,
singing new songs from strange lands?

Or do they just eke out brief lives
"amid the alien corn", and die as
sad and lonely exiles?

Or do they wait, in hope, until another
of their kind (but not their gender) blows in,
as they did, to become a mate and settler,
co-founder of a dynasty?
And the twitchers lose interest.

# HOW THE BIRDS OF PARADISE BECAME BEAUTIFUL
*A Story*

It is said that when God made the birds, he had so much beauty left over when he got to Papua New Guinea that he offered it all to the Birds of Paradise who lived there. They were rather dull in appearance in those days, as the females still are.

The females declined the offer. They knew that being a bird with very beautiful plumage is a bad idea, for two good reasons.

Firstly, it makes you conspicuous and so more likely to fall victim to predators. And secondly, human beings will hunt you for your spectacular feathers and wear them themselves, because human beings have no such beauty of their own.

But the males wanted to be beautiful anyway – so they could show off, strut their stuff, and generally cut a dash in the gloomy forest.

But when God offered them so much beauty, they couldn't decide which pieces of gorgeous plumage to choose. They argued, they hummed and they hawed, they kept changing their minds. In the end God got fed up and just threw the whole lot over them.

And that is why the male Birds of Paradise are such a riot of beauty to this day.

*(continued overleaf)*

And human beings do hunt the male birds for their
spectacular plumage, just as the females warned. But that
hasn't stopped the females from admiring the beauty anyway.
They just can't help it!

No one can!

## ALDEBURGH, LATE NOVEMBER SUNDAY

Out from the High Street chapel
where thirty souls reflected on Beatitudes
and heard the living, saving Word ...

... the lifeboat coming home across the North Sea swell
and crunching up the beach – brave saviours of lives
and maybe souls as well ...

... white gulls sitting on fishermen's black huts
with watchful menace, knowing that death
means life – for them at least ...

... The Scallop, declaring that we will be heard
if, amidst the tempest, we persist in living ...

... and over all an arching rainbow, to which,
like Wordsworth's, my heart leaps up
to feel a blessing.

[Note: The Scallop is a sculpture by Maggi Hambling on
Aldeburgh beach, inscribed with a quotation from Benjamin
Britten's opera 'Peter Grimes':
*I hear those voices that will not be drowned.* ]

# TOO HOT? ADVICE IN A HEAT WAVE

*I got a heat wave burning in my heart.*
(Martha & The Vandellas, 'Heat Wave', 1963)

*And they heard the voice of the Lord God*
*walking in the garden in the cool of the day.*
(Genesis 3: 8)

Too hot to move?
*Don't move.*

Too hot to run?
*Don't run.*

Too hot to walk?
*Don't walk.*

Too hot to work?
*Don't work.*

Too hot to go to bed?
*Don't go to bed.*

Too hot to sleep?
*Don't try.*

Too hot to put your clothes on?
*Don't put your clothes on.*

Too hot to keep your clothes on?
*Take them off.*

Too hot to dance?
*It's never too hot to dance!*

# DO YOU REMEMBER ELEPHANTS?
*A 22nd-century conversation*

"Do you remember elephants, Grandpa? We saw an old holo-projection about them at school today. About Africa in the olden days.

There were rhinos and lions and giraffes too. Do you remember them? They all used to live in Africa, where the big deserts are now. There were a lot of people there too, in those days – and farms and cities!

Did you ever go to Africa, Grandpa, when people still could? When lots of it was still covered with jungle and – what was it they called it? – savannah?

The projection said that there haven't been any big animals there – or anywhere – for a long time. And the people had to leave too – those that could. The rest died, it was horrible!

You are very old, Grandpa! Did you ever see them, those animals? Maybe you saw them here, in those places where they tried to keep some alive for a while? Zoos, they called them, I think. But there just weren't enough and they all died in the end. Did you ever see them?"

"No, I'm afraid not," said Grandpa. "I'm not that old! But *my* Dad remembered seeing them. And when he talked about them, he had tears in his eyes."

# ON NATURE'S SIDE

When we were boys in the North,
my brother and I, and we still had
the courage of our deepest green convictions,
we used to trespass on the grouse moors.

We didn't recognise the property rights
of those who claimed to own them and who,
in our eyes, so misused their 'property'.

Gamekeepers and their employers
were the enemy, along with all those
whose pleasure it was to blast away
at anything that moved over the heather.

We were on Nature's side:
the side of both prey and predator,
the side of grouse and the side
of the hawks and harriers who hunted them
in fulfilment of the eternal cycle.

But the enemy dealt out death, and only death,
to predator and prey; killing, not to eat
but for killing's sake; taking pleasure in destruction.

And so we trespassed on the moors
with righteous indignation,
'scent-marking' the shooting butts
as we passed them by.

And maybe, given the chance,
I still would!

## TO AN ANT
*Fynn Valley, Suffolk, September*

Sister ant –
selfless, industrious,
dedicated without reserve
to the common cause –

Why can't we learn
a lesson from you?


## COLOURS OF THE RAINBOW

*My bow I set in the clouds to be a sign of the covenant
between myself and the earth.* (Genesis 9: 13)

Rainbows have become our symbols of hope,
our defiance of the pestilence that spreads fear,
ruin, and death around our world.

What can be the meanings of those seven colours?
The meanings we could give them as a prayer,
as an affirmation of the life we cherish?

Let red be for the courage and devotion of those
who risk their lives to protect and heal us.

Let orange be for the warmth of their compassion,
for the inner flame that fires their resolution.

Let yellow be for the exultant spirit in all loving hearts,
shining undefeated like the golden sun.

Let green be for the earth, for resurgent nature,
for the springtime beauty that refreshes our weariness.

Let blue be for transcendence, for the over-arching sky
that lifts us up when we are weighed down.

Let indigo be for quietness and reflection,
for the soul's rest and restoration.

Let violet be for our mourning and our grief,
the beauty that is loving sorrow.

The rainbow can encompass all our moods,
all our colours, all shades of our glorious diversity.
And may it stand for the assurance that all will be well.

# SEASONS

## THE CLARITY OF WINTER

The Old Year and its turning is behind you.

In the spareness and clarity of winter,
see the promise of a New Year.
Sense the possibilities forming within you,
feel the silent stirring of life beneath your feet.

The nights are still long, but they're getting shorter.
The days are still dark, but they're getting lighter.
Nature still seems to sleep, but she is awakening.
Winter is preparing the earth for spring.

Give thanks.


## EASTER 2020
*From midday a darkness fell over the whole land.* (Matthew 27: 45)

*The angel spoke to the women: "You have nothing to fear. He has
been raised." They hurried away in awe and great joy.*
(Matthew 28: 5–6, 8)

*There was another horse, sickly pale; its rider's name was Death.*
(Revelation 6: 8)
*A white horse appeared; its rider's name was Faithful and True.*
(Revelation 19: 11)

*Winter gray and falling rain
We'll see summer come again.*
(The Grateful Dead, 'Weather Report', 1973)

.

It was a time of failing hope;
a time of betrayal, despair, and darkness at noon;
a time when fear and death seemed to triumph.

There have been many such times.
Times when it seemed that the pale horse and its
ghastly rider might drive life from the earth.

Maybe we live in such a blighted time,
even though we are surrounded
by springtime flowers and bursting buds.

There is a shadow over the world,
robbing us of the season's joy,
mocking its beauty.

But though we must not diminish
the dangers we face, let us remember
that death never has the last word.

The faith of Easter is that beyond darkness
there is light, beyond sorrow there is joy,
beyond death there is life.

We are called to be messengers of hope
and compassion to each other,
to our neighbours and to the world.

When the crisis passes, may each of us be able
to reflect that we didn't altogether fail the test
of love, conscience, and humanity.

*(continued overleaf)*

We are living through a bitter, fearful spring,
but it will come to an end, and we'll see
summer come again.


## GREENWOOD
*Captain's Wood, Suffolk, May*

There are days when it's worth getting wet,
and this is one of them.

No leaves can be so fresh
as those that open here today,
dripping with raindrops
as bluebells unfold their fragrant carpet,
and sweet-scented gorse blazes yellow.
Small birds make melody, as they did
for Chaucer and his springtime pilgrims.
A muntjac springs away, and fallow deer
watch me, moving warily among the trees.
This is the greenwood of England's dreaming,
the greenwood of Robin and Marian;
the eternal forest that waits for us to leave
so it can spread again across the land,
as one day it will.

There are days when it's worth getting wet,
and this has been one of them.

# MIDSUMMER

*Long ago in the quiet of the world, when there was less noise and
more green ... it was a midsummer's morning as fair and fresh
as could be dreamed: blue sky and never a cloud, and the sun
dancing on the water.*
(J.R.R. Tolkien, *The Hobbit*, 1937)

We greet midsummer –
the dream of endless days and short warm nights,
when our ancestors danced in honour of the sun
and the season's triumph.

There was gladness then beneath blue skies,
hope of plenty as crops grew and ripened in the fields,
food for people and their animals; when there were
feasting and festival to mark the sacred time.

We live too far apart from the turning seasons,
the earth's rhythms and nature's lessons.
We forget our dependence on the plenty
that we take for granted – few of us plant the seed,
watch growth and ripening, reap the harvest.

At midsummer may we open our eyes
to the same life-giving beauty
that our ancestors knew,
our spirits to the call to cherish it,
our minds to the knowledge
of our reliance on earth's bounty.

At midsummer let's celebrate!

## FIRST CONKER
*Fynn Valley, Suffolk, September*

What is it about the first conker of autumn
that makes me stop to pick it up,
feel its rounded, smooth unevenness,
look into its richness of colour,
its mazy, contoured whorls?

This was the currency of boyhood,
in tournaments that tested it to destruction,
but now I use it for nothing.
It is inedible and impractical; a danger,
the dullards say, to 'health and safety'.

But to me the first conker,
like all the rest, is a thing of beauty.
I give thanks for it
and for my capacity to see it so.

## ANOTHER AUTUMN

Another autumn.

Another season of melancholy
and remembered loss.

Another season when Nature teaches us
that we are mortal.

Another time when we know that we are travelling
on a one-way ticket.

Another season when beauty mingles with tears.

Another autumn.

## GOLD
*Fynn Valley, Suffolk, November*

Why do we value gold?
The metal, that is, and not the maple leaves
that fall around me, bringing beauty
and richness to the living earth.

We can't eat it when we're hungry,
we can't wear it when we're cold;
all it really has is beauty, and that we lock
away unseen in vault and strongroom.

So there's another question:
do we really value gold?

## AT HALLOWE'EN
*31st October 1969*

At Hallowe'en
the barriers between life and death,
the living and the dead,
grow thin and porous:
the spirits reach through,
pass through, touch again
until the night ends –
then the barriers solidify
once more.

One Hallowe'en
half a century ago tonight,
I approached the barrier,
passed through it, but returned;
the Reaper relented.

Tonight I remember that night –
although I don't remember it at all –
but I know it happened.
My life was suspended
for a week, maybe two,
then, stuttering back,
resumed its course.
But it was a new course,
and the world became a different place.

## CHILDREN IN THE GARDEN OF REMEMBRANCE

*'The Good Shepherd's Garden', Ipswich Old Cemetery*

A bright November morning:
poppies on wooden crosses,
crosses clutched by children,
children brought to remember, to remember
men they couldn't possibly remember,
men who died a century ago in a war
so terrible I cannot forget it,
though I don't remember it.

What do they think, those children,
what do they make of the bugles,
the poetry, the silence?

When I was a child, we too 'remembered'
the dead of two world wars, the wars
our parents and grandparents had fought in,
lived through – or not. But we didn't
'remember' the dead of Crimea,
the soldiers of a hundred years before.
How could we 'remember' them?
They'd been dead too long.

And yet children today are brought
to 'remember' the dead of a hundred years ago.
Haven't *they* been dead too long?
What do those children think?
Who do they 'remember'?

*(continued overleaf)*

What will their children's children
'remember' if they stand here
a hundred years from now?
And who?


## POPPIES

*In Flanders fields the poppies blow*
*Between the crosses, row on row.*
(John McRae, 1872–1918)

I have always worn a poppy at Remembrancetide,
a red one, and only a red one.

Red, like the poppies my grandfather saw
in war-torn France a hundred years ago,
as his comrades died around him;
red, like the poppy he always wore on Remembrance Day,
his tough old soldier's eyes filled with tears.

In remembering the dead of war,
my red poppy stands for peace,
as his did – the peace which
the dead of war, and its survivors,
wanted more than anyone.

I wear a red poppy, not a white one,
because white poppies are the ancient symbol
of a drugged forgetting,
a false narcotic reverie.

I wear a red poppy because it is earthed
in blood-soaked battlefields, where the dead
cry out for us to remember them, to work for the day
when all such battlefields are green again,
when war shall really be no more,
 and peace will turn from pipe-dream to reality.

## LATE AUTUMN MEDITATION

Autumn falls into winter,
its beauty drifting down
to be a carpet for the drowsy earth.

It is a time of remembrance -
for all saints and all souls,
for all the dead of war,
and for all the dead of peace.

It is a time to remember those once close to us
who have lived their lives
and then surrendered them
to the Great Mystery whence they came.

It is a time to remember the friends
we never see, the lovers we have lost,
the unforgotten who blessed our lives
with theirs, then faded into memory.

*(continued overleaf)*

And as November weeks pass into December,
shopping-streets begin to gleam and glitter,
and twinkling trees appear in front-room windows,
town-hall squares.

And Advent comes, then Christmas,
and perhaps we will remember then
the coming of the Christ-child.


## THE DULL FACTUALIST AT CHRISTMAS

*"Now what I want is Facts. Teach these boys and girls nothing but
Facts. Facts alone are wanted in life."*
('Mr. Gradgrind' in Charles Dickens' *Hard Times*, 1854)

*"What images do I associate with the Christmas music ...? An
angel speaking to a group of shepherds in a field; some travellers,
with eyes uplifted, following a star; a baby in a manger..."*
(Charles Dickens, from *A Christmas Tree*, 1850)

The dull factualist will tell you that there was no star, no
shepherds, no wise men – let alone kings; that there was no
inn, no stable, no manger; that there was no donkey, no oxen,
no camels, and no baby either. Or if there was, he wasn't born
in Bethlehem, his mother wasn't a virgin, and the Holy Spirit
(whatever that is) had nothing to do with it. And the dull
factualist will insist that there were certainly no angels to sing of
Peace and Goodwill, calling us to enter God's Kingdom and build
a better world.

And maybe the dull factualist would be right, as anyone who has studied these things will tell you. But, do you know, the dull factualist is also wrong.

The truth of the Christmas story doesn't lie in dull facts. It lies in something the dull factualist doesn't understand and cannot grasp. Whatever the 'facts', whatever happened *then*, Jesus is born *today* in a Bethlehem of the heart – a baby who is attended by the heavenly host, the shepherds, the wise men, and all the rest. They rise from memory and imagination to bless and guide us at this sacred season.

Jesus lived – and lives – to teach us how to be truly human, how to love our neighbour and to care; how to learn the greatest fact of all: that within each one of us who is born into this world there is the possibility of rising from the dullness and death of the human spirit to live abundantly, to live for each other as channels of the Love that is Divine.

Merry Christmas!


**GIFTS**
*They opened their treasures and offered unto him gifts, gold, frankincense, and myrrh.* (Matthew 2: 11)

This is the season for giving and receiving gifts
in remembrance of the gifts
given by the Magi to the newborn king,
in celebration of God's gift to us of the humble saviour
and his good news of the newborn kingdom.

*(continued overleaf)*

As we exchange gifts this Christmas,
may we learn that a gift, given in love,
is more than the gift itself;
it is more even than the thought that went
into its choosing, its wrapping, its giving.

A gift given in love creates a memory
that may outlast both the gift and the thought,
becoming part of the fabric of one's being,
blessing it for ever.

As we remember the gifts of the Magi
to the infant Jesus, we remember God's gift to us
of Christ himself, who trod the path of suffering
to teach us how to love.

## THE MEANING OF CHRISTMAS?

*... as years go on and heads get gray,*
*how fast the guests do go!*
*Touch hands, touch hands*
*with those that stay.*
*Strong hands to weak,*
*old hands to young,*
*around the Christmas board,*
*touch hands...*
(William Henry Harrison Murray, 1840–1904.
'Touch Hands')

What does Christmas mean
when your years grow long
yet seem so short?

What can you do when your old friends
are mostly lost, or even dead?

When there are no more parties,
at least, not the sort that you can enjoy –
or are allowed to?
When the music is but an echo,
and the dancing stopped a long, long time ago?

Well, you can watch the rising generations
do what you once did...
They are on the long journey
from where you once were
to where you are now.
But there is no going back,
and Christmas cannot be for you
what once it was.

But some things don't change:
Christmas is still the festival of Christ's birth,
when a star shines and angels sing,
and we are called to be better
than we mostly are.

That's what Christmas means,
and that's worth celebrating,
at seven, seventeen, or seventy –
so enjoy it! Merry Christmas!

## HUMBLE KING

A humble king
of humble souls
he was.

Born in lowliness
in a world of emperors
and self-appointed gods,
he lived in humility that
was never mere weakness.

He claimed his kingdom
as no other king had done –
without pomp or pretence.
He made no claim
to special blood, to earthly power,
to divinity.

At his makeshift cradle
the wise of the earth gave rich gifts,
bitter with irony.
To his birthplace,
the arrogant of the earth
brought slaughter of the innocent –
as they still do,
fearful that the lie in their hearts
will be exposed, as it always is.

This holy night his sisters and his brothers
are being born in lowliness, as he was:
may their humility never be polluted,
and may ours be restored. Let it be.

## WHAT JOSEPH SAID TO MARY...
## MAYBE!

I love you, that's all that matters.
You don't need to explain to me.

Don't worry what people say. I never
did have time for the spite and hypocrisy
that passes for their religion.

If you say that God is the father,
then that's good enough for me.
We're all God's children anyway.

I love you and I always will.
Any baby of yours is a baby of mine.
You can count on me,
and so can the baby.


## LOVE, JOSEPH, AND THE ANGEL

People say,
"How remarkable that
Joseph stuck by Mary
and took her to Bethlehem
to give birth to someone else's baby."

Well, maybe it was,
in that god-bothered time and place.
But if he loved her, it wasn't so hard.
I was nearly there myself once.

*(continued overleaf)*

The story goes that an angel came to Joseph
to tell him it was all right,
but maybe the angel
was love.


## THE SAME STARS SHINE: CHRISTMAS 2020

The same stars shine on us
as shone on Bethlehem
when Jesus was born.

They shone on the same world
with light that even then was
ancient beyond comprehension.

It was a world of misery and unrest,
beset by war and pestilence,
oppression and bitterness,
cruelty, grief, and pain.

It was a world not so very unlike
our own as we might think.
But there was hope,
shining like the stars,

Shining in a child, in his mother's love.
Shining in his father's tenderness.
Shining in the wonder of shepherds,
the awe of travelling sages.

And there is hope now, shining in human love,
shining in human courage and compassion,
in the human mind turned to good and noble ends,
shining with the Spirit that filled Jesus.

Beneath the same stars that shone on Jesus,
on all great souls, all souls who strive and
struggle on this good earth, we pray to be
worthy of the promise implicit in our birth.

# PASSAGE

# WHAT BABIES ARE MADE OF

*"I'm made up of the memories of my parents and grandparents, all
my ancestors..."*
(Terry Pratchett, *A Hat Full of Sky*, 2004)

You are formed of stardust,
moulded by the genes
your parents have given you,
and which their parents gave them,
and so on back through
the countless generations.

Their thoughts and their experiences
will help to make you the person
you will become – their love and their caring,
their hopes for you and for themselves.

You will be influenced
by the traditions and beliefs
of your family, your culture, your country;
by your education, your friends,
and by people you don't even know.

But you are a free person,
free to live your own life,
and we ask a blessing on it.

# RULES

*"But I thought there were rules."'...*
*"Oh? Really? ... Did you sign anything? Did you take any kind of*
*oath? No? Then they weren't your rules.'"*
(Terry Pratchett, *A Hat Full of Sky*, 2004)

When you're young,
you come up against rules.

There are two kinds of rules.

The first kind is there to protect you,
and other people,
from your own foolishness.

The other kind is the product
of control-freaks who resent your youth
and fear it; who've forgotten
what it was to be young,
or never really knew – so pity them.

Respect the first kind.

The other rules are mostly there
to be questioned, pushed against, gently tested
'til they crack under the weight of their own absurdity.

There are two kinds of rules.
Make sure you know the difference.

## BEING FIFTEEN

*But now I'm not afraid...*
*No, I'm not ashamed, just*
*give me life, give me life, give me life.*
(St. Vincent [a.k.a. Annie Clark], *Bad Believer*, 2015)

Be strong
to make your own way.
Be courageous
against anyone who would trample on you.
Be free
under the sun, it's your world.
Be wild,
but only on your own terms.
Be wise
amidst much foolishness.
Be true
to what you know is right.
Be yourself:
"you ain't no one else".
Be kind
        always, always be kind.
Be fifteen:
you won't get another chance!
And be assured
you are not alone
(except when you want to be).

# WAS IT REALLY LOVE?

*Did my heart love till now? Forswear it, sight!*
*For I ne'er saw true beauty till this night.*
(William Shakespeare, *Romeo and Juliet*, I.5)

Was it really love back then,
when we were young?

All that desperation and infatuation;
all that kissing, snogging, and ...
well, who knows?

All those letters, notes,
and interminable phone calls;
all the tears, jealousy,
and occasional heartbreak;
all the knowing that
you couldn't live without her,
or him, but somehow managing it
all the same – because you had to.
Was it really love?

Yes, it was.

It is the purest, truest love
that blesses us
when we are young;
the love over which we have no control,
the love that is truly ecstatic,
the love that is without calculation or guilt,

*(continued overleaf)*

the love untouched by the weariness
and the cynicism of experience,
the love that isn't complicated.

It isn't the only kind of love,
but when you're young
it's the best.

## THE VINE OF LOVE

*Thou hast kept the good wine until now.* (John 2:10)

Love brings us here,
the love that lives and grows
in two human souls.

Love is like a seed
that is sown and which germinates
in mutual attraction.

It is like springtime growth,
erupting in the bright passion of youth,
the youthfulness of passion.

It faces unforeseen obstacles,
it must overcome tests
and challenges and threatening blights.

It finds new shafts of light
to draw it upwards,
new sources of nourishment,
with its deepening roots.

It bears new fruits and, with care,
yields a rich harvest ...
Love grows old, as fine wine grows old,
subtle in its flavours, its colours;
mellow and yet still intoxicating.

We give thanks for love
and raise a glass to loving union.

## WE ARE STARDUST

*A Hymn for a Wedding* (8.7.8.7.)

Stardust, stardust, we are stardust
Moulded into human form,
Man and woman you have made us,
Now to loving friendship called.

Bless us, bless us, Spirit bless us,
Draw our free souls to your side,
Found our homes on loving trust
and on our true vows freely made.

Faithful, faithful, always faithful
To each other and to you,
For your gifts forever grateful,
Mystic graces old and new.

Wonders, wonders, precious wonders
Call us all to humble prayer –
Growing love from first encounter,
Greening earth with longed-for rain.

## THE TIME OF DISSOLUTION

To live in this world
you must be able
to do three things:
to love what is mortal;
to hold it
against your bones knowing
your life depends on it;
and, when the time comes, to let it go,
to let it go.
(Mary Oliver, from 'In Blackwater Woods', 1983)

In this time of dissolution
be with us, Spirit of wholeness
and restoration.

This is the time of the body's
dissolution, the fragmentation
of the construct that once was
consciousness and reason,
awareness, mind, and reflection.

This is the time of dissolution,
of the soul's flight,
of personality's fading,
of the end of active participation
in this material world.

This is the time of dissolution,
the time to let go
of what cannot be held on to –
but our memory remains,

and our love.
These we give thanks for.
We cherish them as part of our whole selves,
and in cherishing them our wholeness is restored.


## FADING

*To every thing there is a season ... a time to be born, and a time to die.*
(Ecclesiastes 3: 1–2)

Some people go too early, I nearly did,
to the very brink.
There are some people who, maybe,
should never have been here at all.
Some people stay too long, or are kept here
when they would be better off gone.

That's not what I want.
Let me fade away –
gently, gracefully,
and with my dignity intact.

The Reaper and I are old friends.
Though I cheated him once,
I won't do so again.
There is a time to live,
and I have lived.
There is a time to die...

## THERE IS AN ENDING...

*There are three things that last for ever: faith, hope, and love:*
*and the greatest of the three is love.* (I Corinthians XIII: 13)

There is an ending to things ...
There is an end to winter and an end to summer,
an end to planting and an end to reaping.
There is an end to joy and an end to happiness,
an end to sadness and an end to grief.

There is an end to our false hopes
and our shallow ambitions,
an end to our misgivings and to our despair.
There is an end to our fragile beliefs
and our sapping doubts,
an end to our fond illusions and our brittle certainties.

There is an end to our songs and our singing,
an end to our tears and our weeping.
There is an end to friendship,
but only when all our friends have taken the last road.

There is an end to our time together
and to the hour of worship.
There is an end to our lives
and the lives of those we love.
But there is no end to love.

May it be so.
Go in peace,
and with the comfort of sweet memory.

# AMBITION

*These had seen movement, and heard music; known*
*Slumber and waking; loved; gone proudly friended.*
(Rupert Brooke, 1887–1915, 'The Dead', from *1914 and Other Poems*)

I will never know what it is to die young,
to "grow not old".
But I nearly managed it once,
in one of the classic ways
that young men die –
knocked off a motor-bike
at the age of twenty-two,
with love in my heart,
so much love,
and a broken head.

I'm over seventy now,
and I don't much like it,
If I die now, I will die old;
what's the use of that?
Some times I feel a foolish ambition
to reclaim that lost eternal youth,
but no one can tell me how.

## PEACE AFTER SUFFERING

God of our hearts,
bringer of comfort
when we think no comfort can be found,
be with all who mourn today.

Giver of peace after suffering,
we thank you for the final gift
you give us, and which you have
granted to our dear *sister / brother...*

Help us to bear grief's burden,
to bear each other's burdens,
and to find joy in our memories.
Amen.


## IN MEMORY OF A FRIEND
(For G. K.)

*I climb the hill: from end to end*
*Of all the landscape underneath,*
*I find no place that does not breathe*
*Some gracious memory of my friend.*
(Alfred, Lord Tennyson, from 'In Memoriam')

We are here to remember our friend,
who shared with us the joys of youth,
the ties of comradeship,
the stirrings of love –
and maybe the lovers who stirred them;
who shared the faith and the ideals that unite us.

We remember his voice,
that soft accent of the south,
light and ready for laughter.
We remember his words of greeting and good fellowship,
of kindness and of reasoning;
his words of parting.

We remember his music – his playing and his singing;
his songs of loving and of humour, songs of the sea,
songs we sang with him here in this place,
in the pubs we took over,
and in the gatherings we shared...

It may be a long time since some of us saw him
or spoke with him, since we shared those days of delight,
but he never ceased to be our friend,
never strayed from fond memory,
nor does he now.

We have all followed our many different paths,
as he followed his –
finding a new life and new loves on a distant shore.
But today, together again, we recall him to our hearts,
here in this haunt of his youth and ours.

We give thanks for the life of our friend,
give thanks that we knew him,
and we give thanks for all that he meant to us –
and still does.

## WHY REMEMBER?

Is it futile to remember
those you have lost?

Those whose love once
filled your life with joy?

Those you will never see again,
can never see again?

Is it futile to remember them
when it brings such sorrow?

No, it's not.

The pain of remembering
is worth it.

In remembrance they live again
in our hearts.

Their faces, voices, movements
arise from the deeps of memory.

They brighten our present,
even though tears may flow.

Something remains. All is not lost.
Remember.

# PLACES

# THIS IS THE PLACE

*Great Hucklow, Derbyshire*

*There's a place where I can go*
*when I feel low, when I feel blue...*
(The Beatles, 'There's a Place', 1963)

There's a place I came to
so often in those days.
It was a very special place
for me back then.
To come here now stirs memories
of friends and lovers lost,
of hopes and plans for a future
that never came.
Instead another future
took its place, a counterfeit,
where we few who remain
grow old and tired and mortal.

That was never part of the plan.
Our music and our singing
ceased long ago –
our days of fun and earnest endeavour,
our nights of wonder and of loving.
Others have taken our place,
who know little of us
 or of what we did and hoped and planned.
They have their own memories
to construct in this place –
where memories are generated
from the walls and from the earth.
They have their hopes and plans too,

but those will go the way of ours.
We cannot determine our own future,
let alone that of our successors.
It is the love we share here
that really matters, it always was,
and that is for now – this moment –
and, maybe, for remembering.


## THE CARIBBEAN SEA

*Feel like dancing*
*Dance 'cause we are free*
*Feel like dancing*
*Come dance with me.*
(Bob Marley & The Wailers, *Roots, Rock, Reggae,* 1976)

The Caribbean Sea is blue,
not just once but many times over.

To this blue beauty add teeming reefs,
add islands, green jewels over which
I first flew a lifetime ago,
on my way to one life's end.

But blue is the colour of sorrow.
On this Sea there is a stain,
known to its peoples
and those who know their history.

Blood, so much blood, has been shed
in this seeming paradise.

*(continued overleaf)*

The blood of exterminated Arawaks and Caribs.
The blood of enslaved Africans,
struggling to survive and to be free.
The blood of warring, buccaneering Europeans.

If, to you, the Caribbean is just white beaches
and sunscreen, then you don't know it at all –
as it was, as it really is now.

The many-blued Caribbean Sea
can get into your blood,
as it first got into mine a lifetime ago,
calling me back with the rhythm of its waves,
the rhythms of its people's music –
mento and calypso, ska, rocksteady, and reggae ...
JAH live!

## EARLY MORNING, RUNAWAY BAY, JAMAICA

*Sun is shining, the weather is sweet*
*make you want to move your dancing feet...*
(Bob Marley & The Wailers, *Sun Is Shining*, 1973)

*... an angel went down at a certain season into the pool, and*
*troubled the water.* (John 5: 2)

A humming bird flits
around the lush garden.
A storm, to the north,
rumbles westward over
the blue Caribbean Sea.

The pool lies as tranquil as Bethesda's,
awaiting the children's merry troubling
of the waters.

For us, it is a place
of healing and restoration;
we have come a long way
to suspend our busy-ness.

For those who live here
it is different.

Paradise is routine for the
angels who tend it.

## ON MY MIND: THE GEORGIA ESTATE, HANOVER PARISH, JAMAICA

*How can you be sitting there,*
*telling me that you care, that you care?*
*When everywhere I look around,*
*the people suffer in suffering,*
*in everywhere, everywhere.*
(Bob Marley & The Wailers, *Survival*, 1979)

*Georgia, Georgia, no peace I find,*
*Just an old sweet song keeps Georgia on my mind.*
(Hoagy Carmichael, 'Georgia on My Mind', 1930)

Maybe the Georgia on your mind
is a State of the Union, or a country,
or a girl you love. *(continued overleaf)*

But there is another Georgia.
It is green and lush and beautiful,
a little piece of paradise, perhaps.

But if it seems that way,
 it wasn't always so.

Once it was a little piece of hell,
where slaves laboured
under the sun and the lash –
laboured to bring sweet luxuries
to rich English tongues, and wealth
to rich English pockets.

In this Jamaican Georgia, the swaying
sugar-cane was watered with African blood.
Babylon ruled, and this is on my mind.

## TWO HOUSES: KINGSTON, JAMAICA

*There is one question I'd really love to ask.*
*Is there a place for the hopeless sinner*
*who has hurt all mankind*
*just to save his own beliefs?*
(Bob Marley & The Wailers, 'One Love / People Get Ready', 1977)

*... pressure drop on you,*
*I say when it drops, oh you gonna feel it,*
*know that you were doing wrong.*
(Frederick 'Toots' Hibbert & The Maytals, 'Pressure Drop', 1969)

Two houses in Kingston, Jamaica.
One is downtown, at 79 Duke Street.
Steeped in history, it is a monument
to oppression and the enslavement
of Africa's sons and daughters.
Its first name was Hibbert House.

It was built by men who fooled themselves
and others that the evil which they did was good,
with God on their side.

Today this house is called Headquarters House,
and those who work there tell Jamaica's story
and her slow, blood-soaked movement
from slavery and colonialism
to freedom and independence.

The other house is on Hope Road,
as it should be. It was, for a time,
the home of a musician, a "soul rebel",
a prophet who sang truth to power.

He confronted Jamaica's past,
 and her present too, with songs now loved,
listened to, and sometimes heeded,
around the world.

And the world crowds to his house to hear
his story (and maybe buy the T-shirt!),
this apostle of Ras Tafari, of our One Humanity,
and of the One Love that should unite us.

# DANCING TO KALAMAZOO

Glittering in May sunshine,
this city is the real America:
drive-in commerce, fast-food,
and shining temples of self-confident faith
line its processional ways.

The Potowatami people
named this place
for its boiling waters,
but another nation lives here now,
another alien culture for the traveller
to wonder at and understand.

If you would know the real America,
forget those tainted seaboard cities.
Penetrate the secret heartland,
approach the fabled city, and
"with the elephant and the kangaroo
dance your way to Kalamazoo".

# GLASTONBURY

*I was younger then.*
*Take me back to when*
*I found my heart and broke it here,*
*Made friends and lost them through the years.*
(Ed Sheeran, 'Castle on the Hill', 2017)

Tonight, watching those beautiful young faces
at Glastonbury –
glittering beneath their floating banners,
shining with joy as they listen, rock, sing,
and jump to the music,

it occurs to me that, fifty years ago,
I was like them,
rocking to the music of my time,
before their parents were even born.

Tonight, they are young,
scarcely realising their blessedness.
And somehow, by some cruel trick of nature,
I am growing old.

Fifty years from tonight, with its music and its magic,
they will be as I am now – and I will be long dead.

And other young faces will be where they are now,
rocking to the unimagined music of their time.

So it goes.

## LONDON'S SECRETS

Those who patrol London's streets should know
over what secrets they walk,
for who knows what is waiting to rise up
from the chaos to disturb our peace.

Blood is there, shed by Boudicca's warriors,
by executioners at Tyburn and the Tower,
by the twentieth century's bombers,
and by the violent and murderous of every age.

The layers of pestilence are there:
King Cholera and Black Death,
consumption, typhus, and the Pox,
along with the Londoners they swept away...

swept into overcrowded churchyards,
noisome plague-pits, great 'cities of the dead'.
There they lie still, around us and beneath us,
in graves marked and unmarked, known and forgotten.

Bazalgette's drains are there,
that kept 'The Stink' at bay
when ancient sewers crumbled.
London's 'lost' rivers are down there too,
consigned to darkness until the city falls at last.

There are damp basements where the poor starved;
strong-rooms for the rich (that aren't always strong enough!);
'ghost' stations of the Underground where Londoners sheltered
from the Blitz, whose dim platforms now are empty,
save for the spirits of those who didn't 'mind the gap'.

London's streets are bright under the sun,
but deeper down there is another London,
a darker London, that waits beneath our consciousness
– waiting for the chance to claim us!


## EUROPE

One continent –
One family of nations –
One hope for the future –
Where the past's divisions
are consigned to history
and present wounds are healed.
Where the voices of hate
are silenced by goodwill
and by the voice of true humanity.

The future cannot lie in the past,
the past of petty states and their petty nationalism,
or, if it does, we see it foreshadowed
in war graves by the million,
in Auschwitz.

# MEMORIAL

## THREE SISTERS
*For Charlotte, Emily, and Anne Brontë*

Champion of the women
in between, who inhabited
the cracks in their society,
as she did; whose minds
were as despised as their
gender and their class.

Shy poet of her moorland home,
shy with the wildness of the wild creatures
that she loved; who shattered
the stereotypes of what
a woman could write.

Quiet feminist, gentle Christian,
faithful servant of the God of love;
who knew that his mercy is unbounded,
that his salvation is universal.

Charlotte, Emily, and Anne;
we give thanks for their genius,
for their novels and their poems;
we grieve for the tragedy of lives
cut short, for suffering undeserved,
not just in a Yorkshire village long ago
but also in our world today.

## ENCLAVES OF HELL
*For Holocaust Memorial Day*

The years grow longer since
the Red Army liberated Auschwitz,
the British Army liberated Belsen,
the American Army liberated Dachau,
as one by one our armies reached
all these enclaves of Hell and freed
those within who were still alive.
We've all seen the pictures.

I went to Auschwitz myself once,
thirty-one years after liberation,
on a summer's day. I entered
beneath those cruel and mocking
words, "Arbeit Macht Frei".
I saw the cells, the gas-chambers,
the "ovens". I saw the piles of
human hair, the shoes and spectacles
and prayer shawls of the murdered millions.
I couldn't speak. I didn't know what to say.

Except that it must never happen again.
But it has – in Bosnia, in Rwanda,
in Iraq, in Syria ...

These murderers do the Devil's work, not God's:
the Devil who killed six million Jews;
the Devil with an inhuman face;
the Devil who lurks in all of us
and nowhere else – denying God,

*(continued overleaf)*

denying humanity, awaiting his chance
to reopen Auschwitz and all the rest
of those enclaves of Hell.

We mustn't let him.


## THE TOWER
*Autumn 2014*

Out from the grey fortress
flows the blood-red tide,
filling the moat with poppies
as the crowds surge by –
wanting to feel something,
wanting to feel something
but not knowing what to feel.
How can you know,
when hell is remembered
with such beauty?


## ON WATCHING THE REBURIAL OF
## KING RICHARD III,
*Leicester Cathedral, 26 March 2015*

*This day was our good King Richard piteously slain and murdered;*
*to the great heaviness of this city.*
(City records of York, August 1485)

The victors write the history,
and the Tudors won at Bosworth,
so it is no surprise that they traduced

the reputation of the king they killed;
treated it as they treated his body –
without respect, without honour, without humanity.
But now, perhaps, some justice has been done.
Five hundred years of propaganda
cannot altogether be undone.
Shakespeare's masterpiece cannot be unwritten –
nor should it be.
But today, as the white roses showered
on his casket, "Our good King Richard"
was laid to peaceful rest at last.

## SAINT ANN'S SQUARE, MANCHESTER, 31 MAY 2017
*For the Twenty-two: In Memoriam*

*But don't look back in anger, I heard you say.*
(Oasis, 'Don't Look Back in Anger', 1995)

Balloon-hearts bobbing,
bright in the Manchester sun –
pink, red, blue, silver ...

An ever-growing sea of flowers,
trapped in cellophane;
toys that no child will ever play with.

Messages written on cards
or chalked on the paving stones,
simple, heartfelt, heartbroken.

*(continued overleaf)*

And the people – hundreds,
always hundreds, maybe more,
always quiet, always respectful,
always sorrowful.

Tears are shed, prayers are said –
mourning for the murdered twenty-two,
mourning for the times of hope,
mourning for the future they will never have
– and nor will we.

Love is stronger than hate, we say,
but hate still kills and maims,
still shatters lives as well as takes them,
still perverts human souls, twisting them to evil;
still despises the humanity of St. Ann's Square.

In the church there I left a prayer
for the victims of terror.
God have mercy.

## ONE LOVE ROLLING…

*One Love! One Heart!*
*Let's get together and feel alright…*
(Bob Marley & The Wailers, 'One Love' / 'People Get Ready', 1977)

One Love rolling through the land –
from north to south and back again.
One Love rolling through the land –
wherever there is violence and terror to be countered,
wherever there is hatred to be overcome in human hearts,

wherever there is disaster to be faced and grief to be comforted.

One Love rolling through the years –
embracing all the friends and lovers I have lost,
all who have been dear to me, all who still are.

One Love rolling through space and time –
healing, reconciling, making us One People – everywhere.

One Love rolling through our One World.


## SOLIDARITY
*Chalice-lighting for 12ᵗʰ October*

On this day in 1942,
Norbert Capek, Unitarian minister and martyr,
originator of the Flower Communion,
was cruelly put to death in a Nazi prison-camp.

We light our chalice
to declare our loyalty
to the faith he held
and the Spirit to which he witnessed.

We light it in solidarity
with all good people
imprisoned and put to death
by evil men.

And may we be delivered
from the evil in ourselves.

## IN A TIME OF FEAR

*The only thing we have to fear is fear itself.*
(Franklin Delano Roosevelt, First Inaugural Address, 1933)

*Let any man consider what must be the miserable condition of this town if, on a sudden, they should all be turned out of employment, that labour should cease, and wages for work be no more.*
(Daniel Defoe, *A Journal of the Plague Year*, 1722)

*Have pity upon us miserable sinners who now are visited with great sickness and mortality.*
(Book of Common Prayer, 1662)

*There is no room for fear in love; perfect love banishes fear.*
(I John 4: 18)

In a time of pandemic, when our prayers
should be for the sick and those who tend them
with courage and compassion,
may we not fall into panic and hysteria.

May unwarranted self-concern not blind us
to the needs of others
or lead us into irresponsibility
and the undermining of community.

May we have a deep and active concern
for those in hardship and real danger,
and not inflate our own lesser worries
into unreal terrors.

May we be conscious that fear
can be the greatest sickness,
infecting our minds and spirits,
paralysing our daily lives
and bringing chaos to the economies and networks
on which they depend.

May our prayer be for reason and good sense
that we may face the crisis
with sound knowledge and clear sight.

And may our hearts be warmed and strengthened
with the love that drives out fear.

This is our prayer and our resolve.

# TESTIMONY

# CONFESSIONS OF A NEO-TRANSCENDENTALIST CHRISTIAN HUMANIST UNITARIAN

*... there is no bar or wall in the soul where man, the effect, ceases, and God, the cause, begins.*
(Ralph Waldo Emerson, 'The Over-Soul')

I am Neo-Transcendentalist because the spirituality and insights of the original Transcendentalists resonate within me: their affirmation of a single seamless Divinity reaching out from our inmost being to the "starry heavens above"; of the inner soul's identity with the universal 'Over-Soul'; of the connecting sacredness indwelling Nature and ourselves, enabling us to experience it as wonder and beauty.

I am Christian because the life and teaching of Jesus is the model I was brought up to follow, and because I see in him and his true disciples the Way to follow still.

I am Humanist because I believe that our human life is the only arena in which to work out our own salvation; that the 'supernatural' is the stuff of myth or of delusion, or – sometimes – the natural we don't yet understand.

I am Unitarian because I believe that God is One – the source, cement, and soul of the universe; that Humanity is One, a single species enriched by its superficial diversities of culture, faith, and ethnicity; that Life on Earth is One, an evolving interdependent web of which we are part; that Liberty of Conscience is the birthright of everyone, and that loving kindness should be our duty, aim, and practice.

# CHANNELLING THE ZEITGEIST

*My year as National President of
the Unitarian Young People's League, 1967–1968*

It was a year of revolutions, of rebellion against
the 'orthodox', the 'respectable', the 'reputable'.

It was a time when Jesus the radical, Jesus the hippy,
Jesus the friend of all who were disapproved of,
walked out to join us from the old pictures –
long-haired, bearded – and full of love, so much love,
with the Magdalen beside him – flowers in her hair,
laughing, free at last.

It was a time of martyrdom for liberty and justice;
a time when we demanded peace, but didn't get it –
except among ourselves.

It was a time when colours danced to such music
as our elders didn't understand
 – and we didn't want them to –
it was ours!

It was the summer when we could love
 – and make love – without guilt,
without fear, without the old ties, the old lies...

We took responsibility for our world, or tried to,
claiming precedence over petrified establishments.
"The times they are a-changing", someone sang.
And we sang a lot, and danced.

*(continued overleaf)*

I was in my dreamtime,
the time of lovers and friends
who shared the dream –
or so I hoped, for it was
a time of hope.

This was the spirit of the times
and it was my spirit,
the spirit I tried to bring
to the people I loved,
the people who, for that magical year,
had chosen me to lead them.

## ZENITH

*Watched the first manned landing on the Moon ... by Neil Armstrong & Buzz Aldrin.* (Diary entry, 20 July 1969)

Not until a human being steps out
on to the surface of Mars
will that moment be equalled –
the moment when Neil Armstrong
and humanity stepped out on to
the surface of the Moon.

That was the zenith
of our adventure
as the human race.
Everything since
has been anti-climax
and retreat.

I count myself fortunate
that I lived to see it;
to see it with a girl I love;
to see it before the Reaper
came calling for the first
time – and the second.


## EARTHRISE: CHRISTMAS 1968

*In the beginning God created the heaven and the earth.*
*And the earth was without form and void...*
(Genesis 1: 1)

*I look at the world and I notice it's turning*
*While my guitar gently weeps.*
*With every mistake we must surely be learning,*
*Still my guitar gently weeps.*
(The Beatles, 'While My Guitar Gently Weeps', 1968)

It was Christmas,
the Christmas when we first saw Earthrise
and heard the opening words of Genesis
being read from somewhere over the Moon.
Our beautiful blue planet
rebuked us for our pettiness,
our stupidity, our worship of false gods.
I was in love back then,
so deep in love that nothing
else seemed to matter,
but my lover and I saw Earthrise,
and I will remember both
until the day I die.

## ROADS

*How many roads must a man walk down*
*before you call him a man?*
(Bob Dylan, 'Blowin' in the Wind', 1963)

When I was young there were many roads
I could have taken,
many I started on but then abandoned.
Some I never took at all, I just left them until,
some day, it chanced that
I should come that way again,
although I never did.

I took some high bright roads,
thronged with friends and laughter,
with lovers sweet and song,
enchanted roads through magic lands,
but in the end they all went nowhere,
only a trackless waste.

On one road I lay bleeding,
and its shadow has never
altogether left me.

One road I took because
the time had come, and I have held
to it through the long years.

But none of these is the unknown
road before me now, leading me
into the darkness – or the light...

## THE LIFE NOT LIVED
*31 October–29 December 1969*

The life I had,
the life I had planned,
the life I hoped for,
wished for:

All ended then,
between broken bone
and broken heart.

That life I never lived –
not in this universe.

I have lived another life since then.

A life I never asked for,
a life I never expected;
a life with a different
cast of characters.

A better life, or worse?
God knows!
The God who laughs at our plans...

## MOTHERING SUNDAY

Well, Mum,
it's many, many years since
you left us for paradise.
If such a state of blissful being really exists,
there is no one more deserving
to have entered it than you.

The world has changed,
the family has changed,
since that sad April day
when we lost you.
I remember your face,
I have photos to remind me;
I remember your words,
but I can't quite recall your voice –
once so familiar, so every-day,
but unheard for so, so long.
The memory must be there,
but I can't reach it,
can't unlock it from its oubliette.

But I remember your love,
I remember your gentleness;
I remember your chips,
your cakes, your Sunday lunches
and your Christmas dinners.

I remember how fiercely
you defended us if we were threatened.

I remember, too, times when we

hurt you with our thoughtlessness
and ingratitude – but it was never
because we ceased to love you,
we never did, we never have.

And love is all we can send you now,
so many Mothering Sundays
since you left us.


## POTATO PICKING

It was 1950s Yorkshire,
in the West Riding, as we called it then,
and come the autumn half-term
it was potato-picking time.

Off we went to the muddy October fields,
pulling the reluctant harvest
from the clinging earth.

We were a willing band,
we nine- and ten-year-olds,
for all the chapped hands and aching backs.

We were earning money,
and, with Bonfire Night just around the corner,
we needed it.

How else to arm ourselves
with all those bangers
and rockets and jumping-jacks
that our parents disapproved of?

## THE KITCHEN
*Hibbert House, 102 Albert Street, Camden Town,*
*London NW1, 1970–1972*

We gathered there each night,
wherever we'd been,
whatever we'd been doing,
to talk and talk and talk the world through –
drinking hot chocolate,
eating toast, and always changing,
changing, changing.
Over the night hours, over the weeks
and months and years
that we were in that kitchen
the 'we' was never quite the same,
an ever-shifting company,
male and female, of many faces,
many voices, views, beliefs,
of diverse allegiances in politics and football.
We were friends, or strangers
who became friends around
that kitchen table, for one night
or for many. There was a night
when I first became a part of it,
there was another night when I left it,
but the kitchen carried on
until the House itself was
lost to London's changes.
There are times when I wish
I was back there,
drinking hot chocolate and eating toast
as we talk into the night.

## EVER BEEN HOMELESS?

*How does it feel? How does it feel?*
*To be without a home*
*Like a complete unknown ...*
(Bob Dylan, 'Like a Rolling Stone', 1965)

Ever been homeless?
I have – not for long,
but long enough to know
what it feels like to be thrown out
on the street on a winter's night
with nowhere to go.

Our pub gave us shelter for a few hours,
laden as we were with luggage and shock –
saved us from the cold
and the indignity.

The first night we slept on the floor
of someone's sister's flat,
a girl I didn't know.

The second night we got back into
the house we'd been thrown out of
and slept there in defiance of the law
and those who'd made of themselves our enemies.

The third night? By then we'd found
a flat – damp and a rat's racecourse,
but a roof we could afford, just,
as only one of us had a steady job.

*(continued overleaf)*

Because our friends came to our aid
with food and drink, we managed.
We weren't homeless and destitute
any more – but I've been there.
Not for long, but I've been there,
and it terrified me.


## UNICORNS, DRAGONS, AND MERMAIDS

*Somewhere, all stories are real and all dreams come true.*
(Terry Pratchett, *The Wee Free Men*, 2003)

*... We sing of ecstasy,*
*Of warmth, of love, of passion,*
*Of flights of fantasy.*
(Deane Starr, 'We Sing the Joy of Living', 1965)

Are there unicorns?

Of course there are! I've seen them,
long ago, the white ones with invisible horns,
searching for a pure maiden –
but I got there first!

Are there dragons?

Of course there are! Why else would
there be dragon-hounds – so tall,
so fire-resistant, so stealthy?
You can only see them out of the corner
of your inner-child's eyes.

Are there dragon-hounds?

Of course there are! You can get one
after a night on Transylvanian plum brandy.
That's when I got mine.

Are there mermaids?

Of course there are! I used to see them
in shabby seaside towns,
with their forked blue denim tails.
They were perilous to meet – but worth it!

You say these things aren't real,
but maybe you should adjust your mind:
there is a fault in your reality.

Mine is more fun!

## ON LISTENING TO EMMYLOU HARRIS

A voice ethereal,
half heard
in a moment of ecstasy,
an intimation
(I hope!)
of the choir invisible.

# INDEX

Lightning Source UK Ltd.
Milton Keynes UK
UKHW010655180421
382158UK00001B/14